HOLDEN VILLAGE
"A Place Apart"

IMAGES

&

REFLECTIONS

Holden Village, "A Place Apart"

Published by:

Bad Burro Press, an imprint of
Catalyst Publications, Inc.
PO Box 2485, Kirkland, WA 98083

catalystpublicationsinc.com

Printed in the United States of America
First Printing 2019

ISBN 978-1-943783-06-9

HOLDEN VILLAGE

Latitude: 48.1995639

Longitude: 120.7746736

In March 2019 I had the opportunity and pleasure of visiting Holden Village with Jim Wilcher, a good friend, outdoor enthusiast and talented artist. We heeded the invitation of Alisa and Nick Jeffries, who were residing at the Village as the educational instructor and electrician, respectively.

The hospitality shown us by the Holden staff and volunteers was as sublime as the boat trip on Lake Chelan, the bumpy ride alongside Railroad Creek in the Village's yellow school bus, the nutritious food, plentiful coffee/tea, and the awesome treks along the many trails and up to Copper Basin.

Holden Village is "a place apart" to reflect and refresh amidst an embracing community.

This collection of illustrations, historical references and quotations will hopefully inspire reflections, motivate artistic colorations and, possibly, prompt a visit to Holden Village.

Christopher J. Fox

"The mountains are calling
and I must go."

John Muir

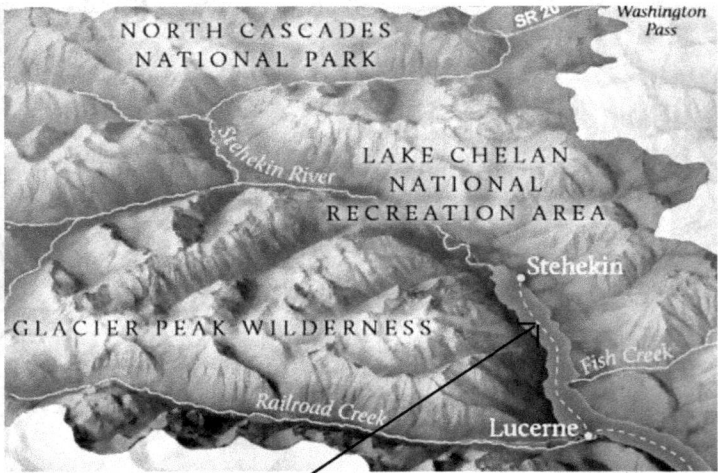

Lake Chelan: 50.5 miles long

Washington State Department
of Natural Resources

Lady of the Lake

Boarding either at Chelan or Fields Point Landing (16 miles uplake from Chelan). Two or four hour ride. Lands at Lucerne.

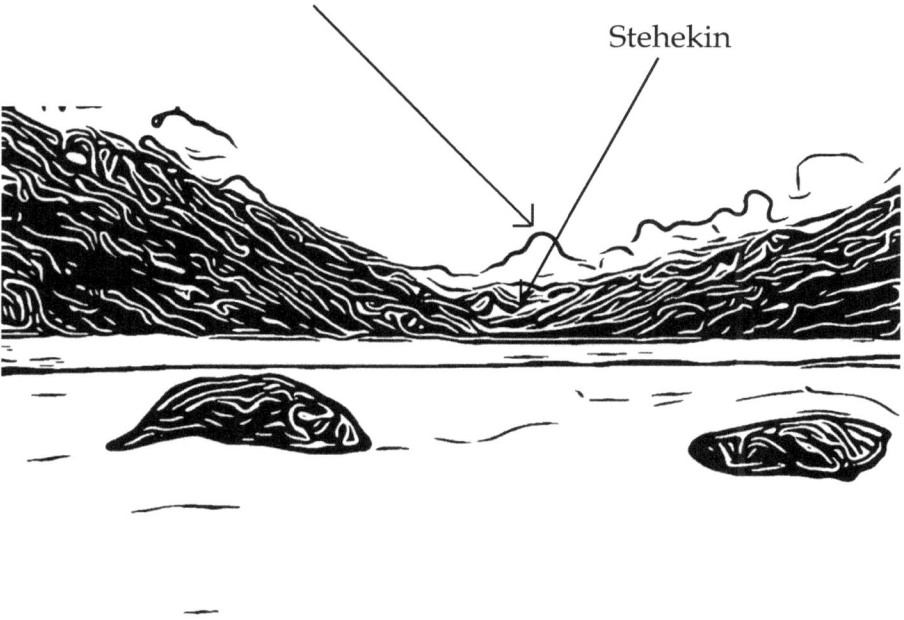

McGregor
Mountain
Elevation: 8136 feet

Stehekin

View from Lucerne Landing
northwest toward Stehekin (*"the way through"*,
referencing the east-west route over Cascade Pass)
and the North Cascades.

Lucerne Boat Dock & Ramp

Camp Gettysburg grocery and post office
(1924-1956)
Lucerne

SECURES OPTION ON CHELAN ROAD

For approximately 5 cents a share J.P. Graves has obtained an option till next July on the 420,000 shares of outstanding stock of the Chelan Transportation & Smelting company. It was agreed among the stockholders that the price should not be made public. It is known that Mr. Graves offered the stockholders 5 cents a share, but that they wanted more. It is understood that Mr. Graves made a slight concession and the price was slightly above 5 cents.

The company has graded about 12 miles of road extending from the properties of the Holden Gold & Copper Mining company to the mouth of Railroad creek on Lake Chelan. The proposed line is about 13 miles long and all but one mile has been graded. The work cost approximately $65,000. No rails have ever been laid.

The Wenatchee Daily World
April 11, 1907

Lucerne
Elevation:
1,109 feet

Holden Village
Elevation:
3,228 feet

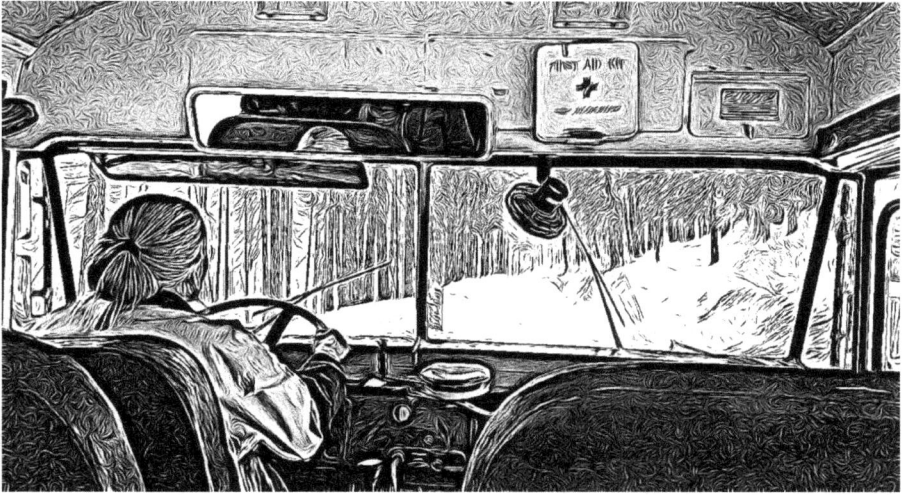

Navigating the road between
Lucerne & Holden Village

11 miles - 12 switchbacks

Buckskin Mountain
Elevation: 8061 feet

HOLDEN MINE IS NOW IN LITIGATION

Superior Court in Session Monday – Jury Term postponed Till August – Cases Docketed.

The question of the ownership of The Holden mine on Lake Chelan will be thrashed out in the July term of the Superior court, which opens next Monday. This mine, the most valuable on Lake Chelan, is valued at about $200,000. Victor W. S. Denny has filed suit against J.H. Holden, Alma J Holden, his wife, and the Holden Gold & Copper Mining Company, asking for an adjudication of his rights in reference to the said mine, alleging that he furnished his grub stake to J.H. Holden previous to the discovery of the mine on the understanding that he was to receive half of the results of his find. This agreement he alleges has not been carried out. The amount involved is in the neighborhood of $100,000.

The Wenatchee Daily World
July 6, 1907

In 1896 Henry Holden founded what eventually became known as the Holden Mine. During its 20 year period of operation (1937 to 1957) it produced 212 million tons of copper and lesser amounts of zinc, silver and gold.

The mining operation ceased in 1957 due to high operating costs and weakening copper demand. The property was eventually sold by then owner Howe Sound to the Lutheran Bible Institute for one dollar.

Remediation of the abandoned mine site occurred between 2011-2016, at the cost of $200 million, paid by Rio Tinto, the mining company that Howe Sound became part of as a result of several mergers.

"Heat, humidity, and dust are the enemies of the copper miner. ... Water coming into contact with sulphide ore generates heat and the moisture 'boils off' until the air is saturated with 80 to 90 per cent humidity."

The Coolidge Examiner,
(Coolidge, Ariz.)
September 7, 1939

"Copper miners know that President Roovelt reduced the price of red metal from 17 to 9 cents a pound and that Leon Henderson, defense commissioner has threatened copper manufacturers that, if a price rate is made, the President, by executive order, will abrogate the 4-cent excise tax on foreign-produced copper, thereby cutting the wages of miners.

VOTE FOR AMERICA! VOTE FOR WILKIE!
VOTE TO UPHOLD YOUR PERSONAL FREEDOM!

The Cooledge Exminer (Cooledge, Ariz.)
October 31, 1940

Kerosene Lantern
[commonly used in mines]

Passenger car on mine railway

Holden's K-12 public school for the children of village's residents, volunteers and staff.

"As children, we are very sensitive to nature's beauty, finding miracles and interesting things everywhere."

Ansel Adams

GOOD FOOD FROM THE GOOD EARTH

our LOCAL FOOD Producers

"Whenever we seek peace and silence, we can retreat to nature. In nature, our senses, minds, and souls are purified."

John Burroughs

One of two vintage (and operable!)
Bombardier snowcats
at Holden Village.

Holden Village
HC 0 Box 2
Chelan, WA 98816-9769

Immediately!
KITCHEN and
DINING HALL

Excellent Opportunities
for Working Couples!

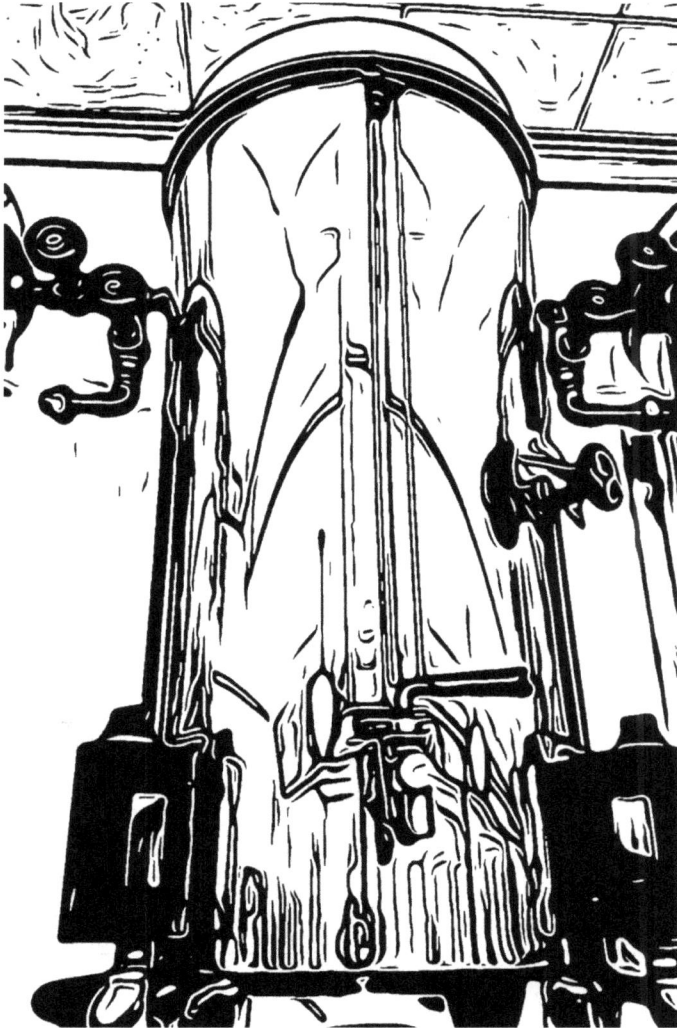

Coffee Urn: "comprising a cylindrical body pro-
vided with a bottom in which is formed a chamber
for the water to be percolated through the coffee.
The body is suitably supported by legs."

Patent Description: 1925

"Music expresses what cannot
be put into words."

Victor Hugo

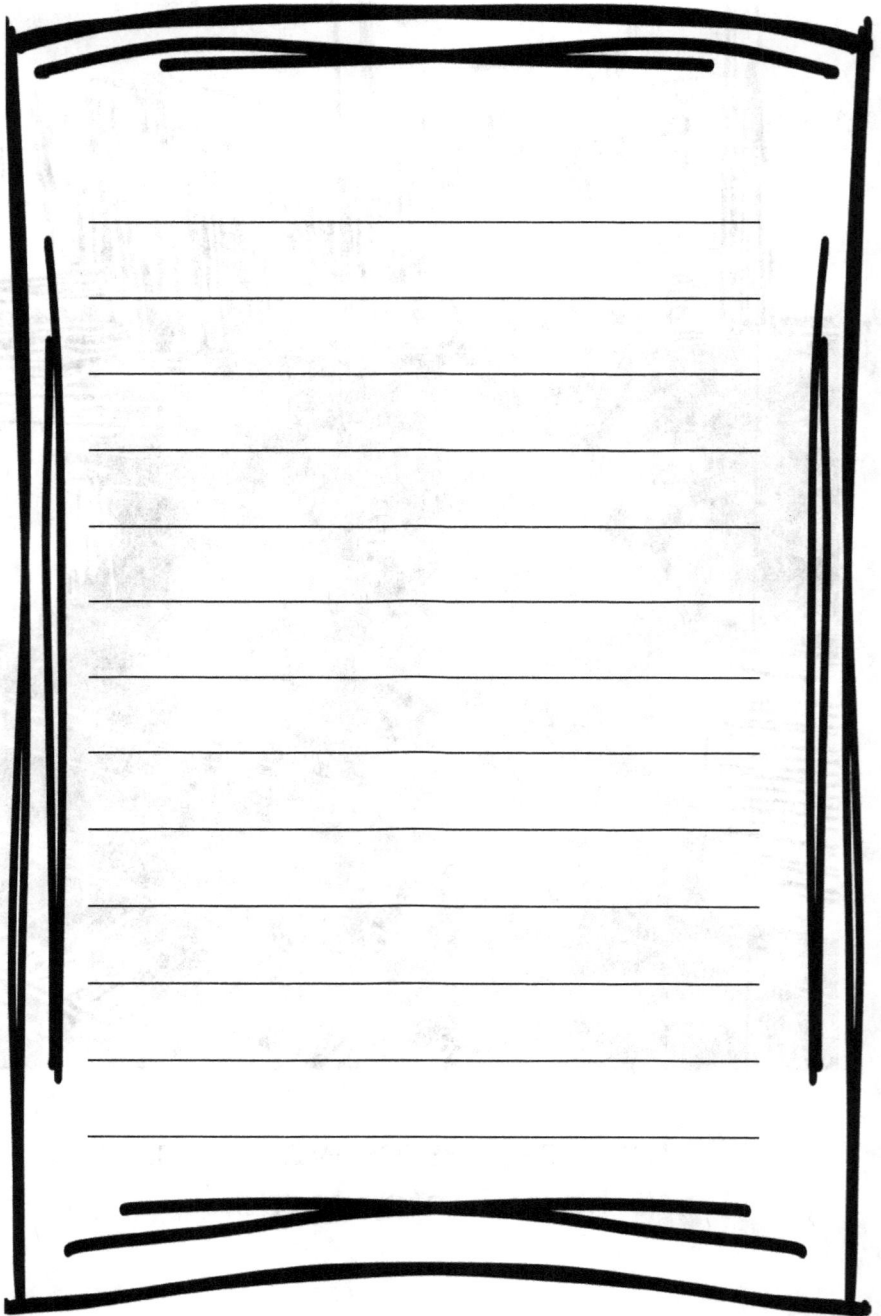

Pool Hall

BOWLING RULES

1. **Wear bowling shoes.** And take them off when you leave or use the restroom,

2. **One at a time.** Wait until the person in the lane next to you is finished before you bowl,

3. **Wait for the pin setter** to signal they are ready,

4. **Be careful to roll the ball** to avoid damaging the lanes

5. **Use the same ball** each time you bowl

The American Flag in the bowling alley.
--
Count the stars!   8 x 6 = ___

Alaska became a state in 19___   & Hawaii became a state in 19___

Buckskin Mountain
Elevation: 8061 feet

Copper Peak
Elevation: 8964 feet

"How glorious a greeting the sun gives the mountains! To behold this is worth the pain of any excursion a thousand times over. The highest peaks burned like islands in a sea of liquid shade. Then the lower peaks and spires caught the glow, and long lances of light, streaming through many a notch and pass fell thick on the frozen meadow."

John Muir, Wilderness Essays

"Nature is full of genius, full of the divinity; so that not a snowflake escapes its fashioning hand."

Henry David Thoreau

"If you truly love nature, you will find beauty everywhere."

Vincent Van Gogh

"At a first glance, nature seems to
follow simple laws that determine
how every process in nature occurs.
This is only an illusion. Nature is not
only complex but also intriguingly
original in every one of its works."

Aristotle

"Taking a walk in nature has healing power for our minds and souls. We don't ask anything from nature, yet nature gives us silence, peace, harmony and beauty, without limits."

John Muir

Remote Washington Village Watchful As Wolverine Fire 'Smolders In The Rocks'

NW News Network, July 14, 2015

Wolverine Fire Continues To Grow, Air Quality At Hazardous Levels

Seattle Times, August 3, 2015

Growing Wolverine Fire Just 1 Mile From Stehekin

Seattle Times, August 6, 2015

Firefighters Backburning To Save Holden Village From Wolverine Fire

NW News Network, August 12, 2015

New Blazes Ignite As Crews Battle Back Wolverine Fire At Holden Village

Seattle Times, August 13, 2015

Holden Village To Welcome Summer Guests Again

NW News Network, May 4, 2017

The 2015 Wolverine Creek Fire threatened Holden Village. The fire started by lightning and burned thousands of acres of forest before finally being contained and extinguished. Holden Village survived. In an Octoer 2, 2017 interview by the The Spokane Spokesman Review, Jeff Marshall, Holden's fire marshall, gave credit to the hotshot crews and a "dome of humidity" created by the just installed high pressure sprinkler system.

"Nature speaks to us through different images, landscapes, colors, patterns, and forms of exquisite beauty. As we admire nature's extravagance, our emotions and feelings become part of it. This harmonious balance makes our souls happy."

Ralph Waldo Emerson

"Since everything is connected in nature, we can observe that nature also has its own support system based on precisely this connection."

Chen Shui-bian

Returning to Chelan aboard
The Lady of the Lake

"We need the tonic of wild-
ness...At the same time that
we are earnest to explore and
learn all things, we require
that all things be mysterious
and unexplorable, that land
and sea be indefinitely wild,
unsurveyed and unfathomed
by us because unfathomable.
We can never have enough of
nature."

Henry David Thoreau
Walden: Or, Life in the Woods